DEAR CLIENT,

DEAR CLIENT,

THIS BOOK WILL TEACH YOU HOW TO GET WHAT YOU WANT FROM CREATIVE PEOPLE.

SINCERELY, BONNIE SIEGLER

ARTISAN | NEW YORK

LIBRARY OF CONGRESS
CATALOGING-IN-PUBLICATION DATA

NAMES: SIEGLER, BONNIE, AUTHOR.
TITLE: DEAR CLIENT : THIS BOOK WILL TEACH YOU HOW
TO GET WHAT YOU WANT FROM CREATIVE PEOPLE /
BONNIE SIEGLER.
DESCRIPTION: NEW YORK : A DIVISION OF
WORKMAN PUBLISHING CO., INC., 2018.
IDENTIFIERS: LCCN 2017047790 |
ISBN 9781579658335 (PB : ALK. PAPER)
SUBJECTS: LCSH: CULTURAL INDUSTRIES—MISCELLANEA. |
INTERPERSONAL COMMUNICATION—MISCELLANEA.
CLASSIFICATION: LCC HD9999.C9472 S54 2018 |
DDC 658.4/5—DC23
LC RECORD AVAILABLE AT
HTTPS://LCCN.LOC.GOV/2017047790

DESIGN BY BONNIE SIEGLER
8POINT5.COM

ARTISAN BOOKS ARE AVAILABLE AT SPECIAL DISCOUNTS
WHEN PURCHASED IN BULK FOR PREMIUMS
AND SALES PROMOTIONS AS WELL AS FOR
FUND-RAISING OR EDUCATIONAL USE.
SPECIAL EDITIONS OR BOOK EXCERPTS ALSO
CAN BE CREATED TO SPECIFICATION.
FOR DETAILS, CONTACT THE SPECIAL SALES DIRECTOR
AT THE ADDRESS BELOW, OR SEND AN E-MAIL TO
SPECIALMARKETS@WORKMAN.COM.

PUBLISHED BY ARTISAN
A DIVISION OF WORKMAN PUBLISHING CO., INC.
225 VARICK STREET
NEW YORK, NY 10014-4381
ARTISANBOOKS.COM

ARTISAN IS A REGISTERED TRADEMARK
OF WORKMAN PUBLISHING CO., INC.

PUBLISHED SIMULTANEOUSLY IN CANADA BY
THOMAS ALLEN & SON, LIMITED

PRINTED IN CHINA
FIRST PRINTING, JANUARY 2018

1 3 5 7 9 10 8 6 4 2

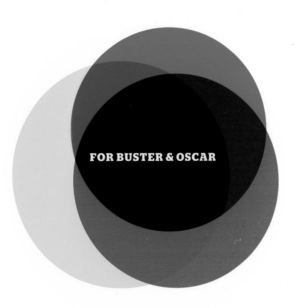

FOR BUSTER & OSCAR

It doesn't make sense to hire smart people and then tell them what to do; we hire smart people so they can tell us what to do.

—Steve Jobs

To design is much more than simply to assemble, to order, or even to edit; it is to add value and meaning, to illuminate, to simplify, to clarify, to dramatize, to persuade, and perhaps even to amuse.

—Paul Rand

There are three ways to ultimate success: The first is to be kind. The second way is to be kind. The third way is to be kind.

—Mr. Rogers

INTRO-
DUCTION

When my first graphic design company, Number 17, was only five years old, Oprah Winfrey (!) hired us to design a book dear to her heart. *Journey to Beloved* combined the diary she kept while making the movie *Beloved* with beautiful photographs from the film shoot. We began the design with trepidation: Honestly, her passion for the book was a huge red flag. Past experiences had taught us that it could be difficult for clients to hear objective opinions from consultants when a project had such deep personal meaning. Plus, there was Oprah's reputation as a demanding perfectionist with enough money to get whatever she wanted.

When we sent her our first pass of the book design, we assumed it would be rejected out of hand or covered with Post-it notes demanding changes without any diplomatic explanation. We waited anxiously for her assistant to call and say, "Please hold for Oprah" or to pass on to us what Oprah thought. Imagine our joy and surprise when Oprah called us herself. It got better: Instead of telling us what to do next, she asked questions about our creative choices. She listened to the answers, and a dialogue ensued. She accepted some of our choices after hearing our explanation and disagreed with others. But because she gave us the opportunity to make our case—and had the opportunity to make hers—the project and our relationship flourished. The book garnered glowing reviews. Most important, Oprah felt that it expressed what she wanted it to, and she cherished the final product. As did we.

If Oprah was an unexpected dream client, another high-profile celebrity (who shall remain nameless) was our nominee for Bad

Client of the Year. The review process began with her telling us she loved the direction, but the next day we received a call from someone who worked for her telling us that the celebrity didn't really like what we had done and didn't really know why. She also asked us to retouch photographs she had supplied in impossible ways.*

Worse, instead of providing feedback we could use to design a second pass, she literally cut up our design and taped it together the way she thought it should look, which made for a mess. We were hamstrung, not to mention tongue-tied. Because it was our job, we continued. We took the elements of her pasteup that we could use and changed things that didn't make sense. Such demands increased the budget, lengthened the schedule, and produced cursing and unhappy people on all sides. After a process this fraught, it's a small miracle that the project turned out as well as it did.

Which kind of client would you like to be?

Whenever designers get together, we complain about difficult clients. We've all had them. Relationships that began with optimism and promise descended into bad feelings. Egos and insecurities are powerful negative forces. Some clients who want to appear smart confuse asking questions with appearing stupid. Or they think they should already know the answers. Others believe that

---

*This happens a lot, and I blame TV and movies. Both industries routinely make it seem like you can easily zoom in on one tiny aspect of a blurry photo and make it perfect instantly. In real life you just can't—but that doesn't stop people from asking you to do it.

since we work for them, we're simply obligated to just do what they want even when we think it is wrong. Still others don't understand the mysteries of the creative process, whether that of architecture, design, copywriting, or a host of other professions that are literally more art than science. All such thinking undermines the creative process and eliminates the opportunity for us to bring our strengths into play.

At the same time, we love our clients. And, of course, we need our clients. You allow us to do the work we adore. A fine artist loves a blank piece of paper with the freedom to do anything. Commercial artists (an old-fashioned term, I know) love a creative brief. I have now owned my own company for twenty-five years, although today it is called Eight and a Half after I split (amicably) with my partner at Number 17 a few years back. (Doesn't the name of my company make sense now?) I still love what I do, all of it: the process, the chaos, the anxiety, and the desire and opportunity to make something great. Sometimes it seems as if we care about the end product more than the client, who may just want the project to be completed. But we often get the most pleasure from obsessing about details that you might not even notice. Of course, I know we can be annoying . . . stubborn . . . irreverent . . . emotional . . . the list goes on. We understand the impulse some clients surely must have to wish they could just do it themselves so they wouldn't have to deal with us.

But you need us as much as we need you. The creative process is not just a matter of giving an assignment and getting a result. There are many phases. Every aspect of the journey needs care and attention. And any collaboration is only as good as the relationships, which take work. I realized long ago that my difficult clients weren't assholes or jerks or stupid. They simply don't know how to work with creative people, and that disconnect consistently leads to frustrations.

That's the topic of this book, the idea for which arose not long after I decided it was time to stop complaining. As Atticus Finch said, "You never really understand a person until you consider things from his point of view."

Ironically, there are many books for designers about how we can better work with clients, which are useful. Most of us want to understand you, so we can improve the process. But, as far as I know, there are no books to help clients better work with creative people, who are a unique species with a unique language and not-so-unique insecurities. Knowing their language and understanding how to talk about subjective concepts is sort of like preparing for foreign travel: You wouldn't go to Tokyo without learning a few words of Japanese. You'd want to be sure you were ordering a dish you could eat and would be able to get back to your hotel without getting lost. This book is meant to make sure you don't get lost in design translation.

I wrote *Dear Client* to teach you how to interact with the creative professional. I approached it from a graphic designer's perspective, but I believe the lessons are applicable to most creative collaborations. I am also writing as a small-business owner. My clients range from entertainment organizations (*Saturday Night Live*) to government entities (the National September 11 Memorial & Museum at the World Trade Center) to Fortune 500 companies (Scotts Miracle-Gro). We are, essentially, a client services company. As such, my goal is to help any client who's ever felt unsure or uneasy with a creative professional feel less conflict, less anxiety, and more joy.

After all, we are on the same side! We want the same thing! And it should be fun! Working with creatives really can be the best part of your day. Figuring out how to create better logos or make your dream kitchen or reinvent your website should be exciting. Together, we are making something out of nothing or improving something that wasn't working. Isn't that more enjoyable than most of your other tasks? Why not bring joy and gratitude to the process?

This book can help your business not only by saving you money and freeing up your time but also by getting you better results. It will also keep your hair from turning gray and reduce the risk of heart attacks.

DISCLAIMER

This book portrays hopes and dreams for ideal scenarios. They rarely occur in the real world, but when they do, it is a beautiful, magical thing. I hope this book serves as a guide for how working relationships can work most effectively. No one is perfect, nor will they ever be, but we can all keep trying.

THE THING ABOUT CREATIVES

NO.

We do what we do because we can't *not* do it. It's how we're wired. It's a passion. In fact, we feel lucky to get paid for doing what we love. But we also feel that clients question the value of what we do way more frequently than we'd prefer. This comes out in all sorts of ways—wondering if our fee was worth the time spent, for example, or failing to pay us—but whatever the manifestation, it's insulting and frustrating.

Creatives are more often than not sensitive souls, a quality that helps us create great work. But this quality also means that **we work better with people who are trusting and positive.** Although most creative work is about problem-solving, it's also about the human connection between us and the client. If you're enthusiastic, engaging, open, and optimistic, we will be too. (To be clear, you can be all of those things and still be a smart, tough critic.) And if you're suspicious, stressed out, and miserly, we may follow your lead. Our defenses will go up, and our inclination to put our hearts on the line will go down. That's not petulance; it's human nature.

BE
HONEST

NO.

We had a client once who loved everything we did. While we were in the same room. The next day, we'd get a call telling us that he'd thought about it and changed his mind. He didn't like anything. It meant that we never believed anything he said when we were together. Which is bad.

Tell the truth. We can take it. In fact, we will appreciate your criticism, even if we don't agree. And if we understand what you're telling us, we'll find a way to implement the changes so they make sense for you, and for us.

And at every single stage of the creative process, **honesty helps more than it hurts** (and it does hurt sometimes). So be kind and considerate and professional and respectful and fair, but don't let any of those admirable qualities keep you from telling us what you really think and how you really feel.

Be honest about budgets.

Be honest about schedules.

Be honest about your company's odd ways.

Be honest about your troublesome colleague.

Be honest about your personal quirks.

Be honest about your boss's priorities.

Be honest about your fears.

BE HONEST

Be honest about what you need to accomplish.

Be honest about your hopes and dreams.

Be honest about what you like.

Be honest about what you hate.

Be honest about what you know and don't know.

Be honest about whom we're trying to please.

Be honest about everything because, truth be told, that's the surest way to get the best work. And the alternative is just a waste of time, energy, and trust.

It's true.

KNOW
THYSELF

NO. 3

Your taste plays a huge part in our work, so you should definitely make an effort to get to know it. Often, when I ask my clients what design work they respond to most strongly, they tell me they've never even considered the question. But everyone has personal preferences, and having a sense of what they are will make it easier to judge creative work with confidence.

Identifying what you like—What tickles you? What pleases you? What draws you in?—will be incredibly helpful in creative collaborations. **The better you understand your taste, the more you'll be able to engage in a useful dialogue throughout the process.** Of course, there may be differences between your personal taste and the needs of your company. A clear understanding of the former will help everyone understand your responses to work done to address the latter.

So before you start working with a creative team, start paying attention to what you like and what you don't like as you go about your day.

Look everywhere: the shelves of supermarkets and drugstores, the street, on television. Don't worry about why you like something, just note that you do. When you're online, focus on engagements that make you smile. Is hitting Facebook's "Love" button satisfying?

Do you respond to oversized images or the simplicity of a scroll? Perhaps you appreciate hidden treats, like the dinosaur game that pops up on Google Chrome's "unable to connect" page (if you don't know about this, check it out). Leaf through magazines, tearing out compelling ads or page layouts. Think of magazines as catalogs of visual eye candy.

Now switch to the perspective of a brand custodian. Look for what you feel are successful representations of a brand; not your personal taste, but a good marriage of product and portrayal. Look for brands with visuals and messaging (pictures and words) that you think work cohesively to make the consumer engagement stronger.

Next, study your competition and determine what's working and, maybe more important, what's not. What makes you jealous? What makes you wonder, What were they thinking? Think about how their design choices relate to your project. Think about how you would respond to them were they presented to you.

Throughout these exercises, keep in mind that you are not looking for potential solutions to a specific problem. You are simply getting in touch with your own aesthetic personality to help us more easily reach a solution that will work for you.

MAKE
ME
ICONIC

NO.

Brands take time to become iconic.

Clients often tell us they want a logo that is instantly recognizable, "like Apple's or Nike's!" What I think they are really saying is that they want to be part of a huge and successful brand effort. What many don't necessarily realize with such entrenched images is that **saturation and time can make a design feel stronger.** That is, you may not have responded positively to the Nike logo in an initial presentation because it didn't necessarily communicate sneakers. You might have asked if it might be more appropriate for a boomerang company. Or maybe suggested that it looked like an odd check mark. But now, after almost fifty years and a cool moniker ("swoosh"), most would say it is one of their favorite logos. Its power reflects an intense familiarity, heroic spokespeople, and many, many marketing dollars.

Think about the New York Yankees logo, which is considered a perfect fit for that baseball franchise even though script typography like that is usually reserved for formal wedding invitations rather than professional sports teams. I don't think the logo is bad, but I am certain it would draw criticism if introduced today. After more than sixty years of use, however, the logo is indistinguishable from the team's identity—and our own emotional attachments.

HAVE CLARITY OF PURPOSE

NO. 5

A clear understanding of your primary business objectives is crucial. And the time to identify them is before you involve us. Seems obvious? I can't tell you how many first calls with potential clients I've had that ended without a discussion of the underlying purpose of the design work to come.

Start by making a list of what you want to achieve or accomplish. Are you trying to increase sales—or make your brand cooler? Do you need your product to stand out on a shelf—or project an image of luxury? Is the idea to increase web traffic—or buzz?

More than likely you will have many dream objectives, but no design can meet every one. Choose the most important one, and then prioritize the others in order. How long should the list be? **If you have more than three priorities, you really don't have any.**

This thinking will be incredibly helpful to whomever you are working with, and they'll think you're amazing for being so organized about your objectives.

Jon Stewart attributed the success of *The Daily Show* and its contributors to "a clarity of vision, but a flexibility of process." That combination allowed magic to happen while a clear focus was maintained. This is a pretty good start for all creative endeavors.

WHO IS YOUR AUDIENCE?

NO. **6**

Before you think it, let me stop you: **"Everyone" isn't an answer.** (You'd be surprised at how many clients begin there.) You must prioritize, and the better you can define your desired audience, the better the creative outcome will be.

So know whom are you trying to reach—and why. Are you targeting people who've never heard of your brand because you're trying to expand? Or are you focusing on those who are already part of the club because you don't want to lose them? Are you trying to connect with the people who decide to buy your product, service, or experience? Or are you trying to reach those who might influence that decision?

If your answers to all of the above are "Yes"—in other words, if you're still having trouble moving past "Everyone"—you might try instead to paint a picture (figuratively) of the attributes of your ideal customer. My guess is that this list will help you narrow your audience pretty quickly. If your desired consumer has disposable income, a college education, and children, "everyone" starts to look like someone very quickly.

After you decide whom you want to reach, figure out why you want to reach them. This will dovetail with your goals, and that's a good thing. Repetition of purpose only reinforces it.

There's one other audience you need to consider:
the decision makers in the creative process. But keep
in mind that those people—you, your colleagues,
your staff, your bosses—are not always in the desired
or targeted demographic. Design is always subjective.
Knowing the difference between your taste and your
audience's taste, as it relates to the solution, will be
important information for you and for us.

CARE ABOUT EVERY AUDIENCE

NO. 7

CARE ABOUT
EVERY AUDIENCE

There are two artificial audience distinctions in creative work, both of which result in less effective solutions. One is business-to-business. For some reason, people think such work should be more straightforward, serious, and, in our experience, less creative and fun. I have no idea why. **B2B consumers are the same people who are also spoken to daily through regular commercial marketing.** They may represent "business" to you and to their employer, but they are humans who are influenced by the same commercial forces as the rest of us—and we should speak to them in a way that shows we get that.

Another artificial distinction involves work done for an internal audience, within a company. Even in companies with tens of thousands of employees, work that is aimed "just internally" is deemed less important. Ironically, it's usually something meant to inspire or teach. It would seem to me that showing this audience that you care is at least as important as talking to strangers.

Every single audience likes to be entertained while being informed, and the extra effort will always pay off.

DECIDE
WHO WILL
DECIDE

NO.

DECIDE WHO WILL DECIDE

A number of years ago we were hired to help create a new identity for the National September 11 Memorial & Museum at the World Trade Center. Understandably, there were many important stakeholders, including the families of those killed, government officials, and the museum directors. Years had gone by without any decisions, until then-New York City mayor Michael Bloomberg announced that he would take on the role of decider. The branding process moved forward smoothly and efficiently from that point on. I am sure some people liked the final design more than others, and that is fine. It really is almost impossible to please all of the people all of the time, so choosing a representative makes progress possible. If no one hates it, most likely no one loves it either—but that's okay.

The plague of groupthink is not limited to creative work, but I can assure you that it is both particularly egregious in—and harmful to—creative collaborations. Because decisions around design, copy, video, and the like are subjective, people with little expertise tend to feel more confident sharing an opinion. And because each person will naturally have unique preferences, any decision made by committee will necessitate compromise and therefore lack singular vision. **Vision is not a group activity,** and the group inevitably interferes with the possibility of greatness.

Choose one person—maybe two—who will be the final decision maker. (Ideally, before we're involved.) Thus empowered, the final arbiter(s) will be more invested in the process and will ensure that it runs smoothly. That person will take their role much more seriously than ten people who each have one-tenth of the ownership.

Such an arrangement doesn't mean that others can't give feedback. In a good collaboration, there is ample opportunity for discussion among all involved. But we'll know how to weigh comments appropriately so that we can progress.

Equally important, make the decision maker's role—and the approval process in general—clear to all players, especially us. Our worst nightmare is a "faux decider." Once, my team went through several rounds of presentations, feedback, and changes before pleasing the person we thought had final say. Only then did we learn about a mystery person who had ultimate approval and an entirely different concept in mind. Had we known there was another layer of approvals, we would have structured our work and our time to reflect this step. Instead, we unexpectedly had to move in another direction. In certain cases, it's understandable that the person making the final call will never attend a meeting. In that case you should tell us who that person is—and who decides what that person sees. We can work with that arrangement . . . if we know that's the arrangement.

DO NOT SEND OUT AN RFP

NO. 9

RFP stands for Request for Proposal, but **I think it really stands for Routinely Futile Paperwork.** Many clients send out a generic RFP because their company requires full vetting of potential vendors. That's totally understandable, but please do not use these RFPs as a way to choose a creative collaborator.

RFPs are just not the way to do that. They're often delivered without the information we need to fully understand a project's scope and type and without dialogue. And they are off-putting, letting us know that this client prefers paperwork to interpersonal relationships. A lengthy RFP—bios for everyone on the project, ten references, pages and pages of case studies—sends a message that we'll be dealing with a lot of bureaucracy. And it doesn't really give you the information you want. We could have a twenty-five-year-old wunderkind on our team whose bio may not impress but whose work certainly will. There is no place for that kind of understanding in an RFP.

More to the point, the person reading submitted RFPs will almost certainly not be the ultimate decision maker. Similarly, the lead creative is not likely to spend their time filling out a twenty-page document. Which means a huge decision is being filtered through people on both sides who aren't the real players. That doesn't make good business sense. If a designer can't convince you that they would be a good fit in two pages, they're likely not going to do it in twenty.

I recommend instead identifying a few firms, researching them (very easy to do on the interweb), and figuring out unique questions appropriate to each firm you are drawn to. Have a thirty-minute meeting with each of them and make your decision based on that.

A BRIEF CASE FOR WRITING A BRIEF

A BRIEF CASE FOR WRITING A BRIEF

A brief is a summary of a project's purpose. It will inform and remind everyone (including you) of the point of the project. (In-house art departments will find the document as valuable as outside creative consultants will.) Basically, it's a synopsis of everything we've just covered: the problem to be solved and the most important goals or aspects to be considered. It's a little more homework, but it will be worth it.

But before the creatives even see it, **it's crucial that key stakeholders agree on the contents of the brief.** Otherwise, everyone will still be debating essential aspects after work has begun. That saps momentum, turns us from optimists into cynics—and inevitably costs you money.

A brief doesn't need to follow a formal structure. It can be a well-crafted essay or a bulleted list. But it should contain the answers to most of these questions:

What is the challenge?

Why are you embarking on the project now?
A LITTLE HISTORY, FROM YOUR PERSPECTIVE, CAN BE VERY HELPFUL.

What are the objectives?

What is the current situation?

Who is the primary audience?

What do you know about them?

What is unique about your product or service?

What three adjectives describe the ideal response?
ANYTHING FROM "BEAUTIFUL" TO "AH, NOW I UNDERSTAND."

What is the schedule?

What are the specific deliverables?

What are the technical or legal requirements?

What else should the creative know?

What are your hopes and dreams?

Yes, the goals may change, which is normal and okay. All creative work—graphic design, architecture, copywriting—is a process, but that process goes much more smoothly if we begin at the same starting point. And this way, no one is relying on their personal (and sometimes mistaken) recollection of what was discussed at the first meeting. It's all in the brief.

TELL ME THE PROBLEM, NOT THE SOLUTION

NO. **11**

What the brief should not do is suggest solutions. That's our job. This is important to remember, because **a proposed direction or solution from a client is often difficult to forget** and may serve to limit a creative team's thinking. You don't want anyone saying, "Oh, they want that kind of solution." The other danger is that we'll judge our ideas against your suggestion and self-edit, which, again, is self-defeating. Your job is simply to communicate your official collection of hopes and dreams.

GET
BUY-IN

NO. 12

Any collaboration will be rocky if your key stakeholders are not on the same page about the project's purpose, intended audience, goals, and budget. And the time to get buy-in is *before* you brief the creative. Whether that means gathering everyone in a room or emailing a document for comments and sign-off, your job as the client is to **make sure that everyone in your organization agrees about the problem that needs to be solved . . .** before you hire someone to craft a solution.

EXPERIENCE ISN'T EVERYTHING

NO. 13

When you call to talk about the possibility of working with us, there are plenty of things to chat about: our process, our staff, our clients, our availability.

Here's a question you shouldn't ask: Have you done a job like this before?

We hear it all the time. Have you ever designed toothpaste packaging? Or, How much experience do you have with websites devoted to interior decorating? In every case, the client is clearly looking for a positive response—and the comfort that comes from knowing we've already solved a problem like theirs. But it's a false comfort at best, for three reasons:

1. The path to every solution should be unique.

That design you like on that similar product? You have no idea what the brief was that led the designers to it or why the client chose the direction they did. How we get to what you need may well take a very different approach. The client is the designer's collaborator, and working with you will undoubtedly be an entirely different experience. It is much more important that you discuss a potential designer's previous work and process holistically. Hear what they have to say about how they came up with the solutions they did—even if none of those solutions have to do with a bathroom product.

EXPERIENCE ISN'T EVERYTHING

2. Obsession with a specific kind of experience displays a lack of imagination—and trust. It also shows an inability to understand the nature of creative problem-solving.

3. Familiarity can breed laziness. Designers who work a lot on one kind of thing tend to offer similar solutions each time. And why not? It pleased a client once, so it should again. But you should want us to do new and different thinking that addresses your specific needs. And not for nothing, for me (and a lot of people like me), work that is too similar to what I've done before just isn't as much fun to do.

That said, experience in a specific area isn't all bad either. It means the designer won't be learning on your job. Back to the toothpaste box: A designer who has done packaging work before will go into the project understanding dielines and bar code restrictions. But the truly important thing is the creativity and the thinking. If the designer is good, they can learn all the logistical stuff to complete your job to perfection, regardless of not having done it before. The thing that they can't google and get an answer to is how to problem-solve creatively.

THOSE AWKWARD FIRST PHONE CALLS

NO. 14

THOSE AWKWARD
FIRST PHONE CALLS

Think of your initial phone conversation with a potential creative hire as the beginning of the collaboration, whether you're considering one firm or ten. **The idea is to sow the seeds for a great partnership from the beginning** by setting a positive tone as you determine if your communication styles jibe.

The best approach is to just talk broadly about your company and your project: tell us how you got to where you are and what you hope to achieve; describe the culture, the people, the approval process. You'll ask questions and we'll ask questions and you'll see how well we communicate with each other. It's just like dating. See if you like the cut of our jib and how we think. See what it's like to have a conversation with us, because if we work together, you're going to have lots of conversations with us. When you get off the phone, you want to be able to answer "Yes" to most of the following questions:

Did we ask thoughtful questions?

Did we listen to your answers?

Did you understand what we said?

Did we seem to understand what you said?

Did we sound like we were responding specifically to you (as opposed to speaking in generic platitudes)?

Did we have the same cultural and/or business references?

If you're not sure what to say to a creative firm, start by asking them, "How can you help us?" Their answer should help you understand what they can do for you.

And pay attention to the questions they ask you. That will help you understand their process, what they need to know. This is a collaboration and, as with dating, you should both enjoy and learn whether you can work together from this conversation.

This is also the time to begin establishing trust (see No. 2, "Be Honest"). So tell us if you're making ten calls before deciding which three firms to meet with (perfectly okay) or if you already know that you want to hire us because you've heard great things (even better). This kind of information is valuable to us—but also to you, since it will help us to determine what to provide you to best assist in your decision.

THE IMPORTANCE OF MEETING IN PERSON

NO. 15

Before you decide to work with a creative team, particularly on a major project, try your best to meet with prospective candidates in person. More so than a call or video chat, this lets both parties see the other in action. You get to read each other's body language. You get to have small talk, which can be the foundation for a (work) friendship. And one of you gets to see where the other works, which obviously can tell you a lot about a person and their organization. Just as crucially, a face-to-face meeting can set the tone for all that's to come. Here's a simple plan sure to get things going in the right direction.

Be prepared.
Know your goals. Arrive with your creative brief in hand; it will help you to articulate the mission. You should also be ready to discuss similar projects you've undertaken and why they were successful—or not. (We often learn more from failure than from success!)

Be optimistic.
Assume success and communicate that assumption. I'm told optimism is as contagious as a sneeze. (Gesundheit!)

Be transparent.
Tell us everything—even the bad stuff, like how the approval process might be a bit of an obstacle course.

Tell us what you know about the timeline and budget too—and the flexibility around each. The more we understand, the better the odds of success, in both product and process.

Be nice.

Sorry to get all basic human decency on you; this is just one of my things. We're all busy and stressed, but we're also all human. So start with a compliment (we, like you, are insecure and needy). You're obviously considering this particular creative team for a reason. Tell them why. You want them on your side, and knowing that you believe in them will help to get them there. (I know I sound like your mother, but sometimes she did know what she was talking about.)

GET A PROPOSAL

NO. 16

GET A PROPOSAL

Once you've spoken on the phone (and, ideally, met in person), ask any potential collaborator for a project proposal. A bare-minimum will include basics such as scope of services, cost, and timetable, but every firm or individual will have their own way of preparing this document—and that's the point. The proposal is another way in which we speak to you, and **it will offer a sneak peek into our working personality:** project understanding, preferred process, level of flexibility, and formality. All of this is useful information when making a decision.

CALL REFERENCES, FOR GOD'S SAKE

NO. **17**

CALL REFERENCES, FOR GOD'S SAKE

We just met and you liked our work and what we had to say and you are thinking of working with us. That may be enough, especially if you were referred to us. But if you just aren't ready to pull the trigger, you are probably wondering what we're *really* like to work with.

Please ask us to give you contact information for a couple of recent clients, and then please give them a call to discuss the experience of working with us. How did the project go? Did we respond well to feedback? Was it a pleasant relationship? Did we meet deadlines? Were they proud of the completed job?

Yes, each project is different, and we probably won't give you contact info for a client with whom we had a terrible relationship. Nevertheless, those with whom we worked well can still provide useful information, especially if you have specific concerns. Maybe you're worried about costs and overages. Ask. Maybe you're wondering whom at the firm you'll really work with. Ask.

And **feel free to come back to us with new questions** based on what you learned. Creatives want to start off on the best foot possible, which means we want you to trust us and not have nagging concerns as we begin this mysterious relationship.

INTRODUCE EVERYONE AT THE MEETING

NO. 18

I've sat at many long conference room tables with absolutely no idea as to who all the people staring at me were, let alone what their roles were or why they were there. And that's not cool, because **if we don't know who's who, we can't be sure which opinions and musings have value.** Obviously, we'll respond differently to a curious decision maker than we will to an intern who's simply expressing a personal preference. We'll be just as nice to the latter but will take more time addressing the concerns of the former.

So who's at this meeting? You tell us. No, seriously—you need to tell us, ideally beforehand. I get it. You may not settle on an invite list until the last minute. But if that's the case, tell us that too. And when we gather, introduce everyone, including the role each plays. Otherwise, all we'll know is that there are a bunch of people in the room who may or may not have names and are definitely there to judge us.

I totally appreciate the inclination to make meetings inclusive. Just include us too.

DON'T SCHEDULE MEETINGS ONE RIGHT AFTER THE OTHER SO THAT WE'RE BOUND TO RUN INTO EACH OTHER IN THE LOBBY

NO. 19

DON'T SCHEDULE MEETINGS ONE RIGHT AFTER THE OTHER SO THAT WE'RE BOUND TO RUN INTO EACH OTHER IN THE LOBBY

I often ask whom else a potential client is talking to. Sometimes they tell me, sometimes they don't. It helps me to get a sense of whom we are up against, but it is not necessary. Running into competitors at the elevator is a whole other thing. I once ran into an ex-boyfriend who was up for the same job. (It's a small world.) He was on the way out of the client's office; I was on the way in. As a result, I was a wreck during the interview, which I spent wondering what he had said and what work he had shown and what his life was like now.

Everyone's time is precious, so we understand how efficient it seems to knock out a bunch of interviews on a single day. But everyone feels uncomfortable and flustered after bumping into a competitor in the lobby— even if they never dated—which means you end up interviewing something other than the best version of what might very well have been an ideal collaborator. It feels a little too much like casting sessions where the struggling actor walks into the lobby and sees twenty other thirty-year-old blond men dressed in jeans and a leather jacket.

And, not for nothing, **meeting potential creatives in rapid-fire succession is not the best way for your brain to process personalities and presentations.**

The best presentation may seem to be the one you saw right after lunch.

So, if you can, space out interviews with time to let all ships pass in the night.

BE
UP FRONT
ABOUT
MONEY

NO.

Creative people are at a little bit of a disadvantage, weirdly, because we love what we do. We feel lucky to get paid for it, and we would probably do it for free. But there are the realities of life, and while we are privileged to earn a living this way, earn money we must. Sure, we like to make money, but for the most part, we really want to kick ass creatively and yes, making money makes it all better. If we were really focused on making money, we'd probably be doing something else.

If you have a specific budget or range for your project, please tell us. **It will make us feel like we're on the same side** (which we desperately want to be) and will avoid protracted negotiations (which can sour the relationship). It will also save everyone time. Some projects are just too small for some creatives, no matter how much they think they might enjoy the work or the relationship—unless you explain that you care passionately about it but don't have the budget you would like. In that case we might just do it!

Some potential clients tell us they have no budget in mind, but there's always a rough number. And in the absence of any guidance, we may approach the project with a proposal that's way more than you expected. That's a quick way to kill what could have been a very rewarding collaboration.

BE UP FRONT ABOUT MONEY

Other would-be clients withhold their budget parameters in the hope that we will bid lower than what they have to spend. But most seasoned creatives don't even want to be the cheapest bidder. Most young creatives, meanwhile, will produce better work if they know you didn't hire them solely because they came in with the lowest bid.

A young colleague was asked to submit a proposal for a job he really wanted. No budget was given, leaving him agitated about having to make a wild guess. He decided to submit a very low bid—he landed on $5,000—hoping that after they saw how awesomely talented he was, he could raise his fees on the next project. The next day he got the job, but in reviewing his proposal and the contract the company sent he realized that in his nervousness, he had accidentally added an extra zero to his fee, making it $50,000—which the client had agreed to.

Maybe $50,000 was less than they planned on spending and everyone walked away happy, but the fact that this designer had *no idea* is absurd. And maybe $50,000 was a stretch for them. If they had just given the designer a range, he still could have come in on the low end and saved the client lots of money.

Having some sense of the budget will affect the way we think about the project from the get-go. Starting out with a mystery between us means there's no way we can be on the same page, which is a terrible way to begin.

Please be up front about money.

THE VALUE OF CREATIVE WORK

NO. 21

A true story: I was once hired to create a new brand identity for a New York City hospital. At one point, the hospital review committee, made up of six male surgeons, assembled to review our initial presentation. While we waited for the CEO to join the meeting, one of the surgeons told a story about a time he felt a designer had ripped him off. Apparently, the organization with which he was then affiliated had spent a lot of money on a new logo. After the work was completed, it was discovered that someone in their office—not a designer—had sketched a logo similar to the one the designer created. The surgeon's point, as I understood it, was that his previous company didn't need a fancy design firm when Johnny down the hall could make the same logo for free.*

I think this story resonates so strongly with me because it hits an issue that we deal with constantly. Because creative work is not easily quantified, some clients question the value of our work. This is not only galling; it also misses the point. **You're paying for our creativity, for our ability to create order from chaos,** to communicate your message, not for the time we need to solve your specific problem. The time it takes is our burden, not yours (so long as we meet deadlines). Is a brilliant logo worth less because we had

*After the fact, I realized what I should have said: "I know exactly how you feel. I once spent a ton of money on this fancy doctor and he could never make a diagnosis, but a neighbor of mine figured it out right away!"

the idea during our initial meeting? Is it worth more because we threw out a hundred ideas along the way?

Whether a solution takes us two days or two weeks or two months, the ultimate value to your business is the same—and that's what you're paying for.

An apocryphal story: A widget factory was brought to a halt by a piece of malfunctioning equipment. Management called a mechanic, who spent five minutes walking around the machine inspecting parts.

Then he pulled something out of his toolbox and tinkered for a moment in the back of the machine, which promptly started to work. Everyone was thrilled, until they got a bill for $5,000. The factory owner angrily asked the mechanic for a breakdown of the costs. The mechanic sent back the following itemization:

$10 for the replacement part

$4,990 for the 25 years of experience that allowed us to solve the problem in 10 minutes

Exactly.

FLAT FEES, FULL HEARTS, CAN'T LOSE

NO. 22

FLAT FEES, FULL HEARTS, CAN'T LOSE

Most designers (and many other creative types) worth their salt charge a flat fee for a project. This may or may not reflect some internal accounting for how many hours they expect to spend on your project, but it certainly includes a rough calculation of the number of people involved for a certain amount of time, their abilities, and the scope of the entire project. Whatever the case, I assure you that this structure benefits you. Here's why: Say my team is designing your logo, and we have an idea that requires drawing a typeface from scratch. If we're charging you by the hour, we have to consider your reaction to spending the extra money, especially if you end up not liking the direction. You would probably not want to invest more money in something that might not even work. If we're on a flat fee, we are more likely to forego such mental calculations and explore even time-consuming options that we think will teach us—or you—something important. **By paying a flat fee, you don't limit us to X hours of work.** The sky is the limit, which is right where you want it to be.

That said, I believe work required beyond the scope of the contract (see No. 23, "Expect the Unexpected") should generally be billed by the hour (at a rate stipulated in the contract). At this stage, hopefully, we will be executing precision strikes to address very specific issues. But whatever the reason, our time has a value and, like a lawyer, we need to charge for the hours we spend beyond what we agreed to. Know that we will work as efficiently as we can while staying the perfectionists you want us to be. To be honest, it's in our interest to work as quickly as possible: The faster a project goes down, the sooner we can move on to new jobs.

EXPECT THE UNEXPECTED

NO. 23

Of course, you have the right to change your mind. (Personally, I think people who never change their minds aren't using them.) As we live with ideas, new thoughts inevitably enter the picture, and that affects the way we see the work. Sometimes a client changes their mind after receiving new information or sharing a presentation with a colleague or just after having a good night's sleep and reviewing it anew in the morning. It happens.

Do we sometimes wish the process were more of a straight line? Sure, but we know why it rarely is, and detours can lead to the best work. Just another reason we find our job so satisfying.

But a change of mind can mean a change of parameters. So every design project—from your annual report to my new kitchen—has the potential to take longer and cost more than anyone anticipated. By definition, **the thing that causes the delay is the thing you can't anticipate;** if you could, we'd have accounted for it in the initial schedule. By all means, think of as many contingencies as you can, but build in extra room for the unknown in both the schedule and budget anyway. (For the latter, an extra 10 percent in the lockbox is a comfortable cushion.)

GOOD, FAST, CHEAP

NO.**24**

The best! Get it now! On sale! Sounds great, right? If you are buying deodorant, this trifecta is great. But with creative projects, **consider yourself lucky if you can get two out of three.** Getting them all is a near impossibility because:

If it's GOOD AND FAST,
more people need to be involved—so it won't be cheap.

If it's GOOD AND CHEAP,
it will take longer—so it won't be fast.

If it's FAST AND CHEAP,
it's probably not going to be good.

ALWAYS SIGN ON A DOTTED LINE

NO. 25

Many creatives have learned hard lessons about the risks of working without a contract. My lesson wasn't even that hard, but it was still educational. We were chosen to design the identity and advertising for Air America, a media brand close to my heart (and politics). We were so excited about the project that we began working without a contract. But we refused to deliver the finished product until both parties had signed, despite a CEO who chided us for not accepting his handshake as assurance . . . like all the other vendors working with Air America had done. Well, we were very grateful for that contract when it turned out the CEO was a fraud and his handshake was worth less than his bank account. That paperwork meant that we were eventually paid in full, while all those vendors who simply shook on it were out of luck.

So please make signing a contract standard practice, whether we're talking about a huge job between two big companies or a relatively small project. I've had many clients—many of them at large organizations— tell me that we don't need a contract. Sometimes it's because they have a little extra money and don't want to call too much attention to the spend. And sometimes it's just in order to avoid the bureaucratic step. I understand this inclination, but it's not a good enough reason to go without. Contracts protect both sides and make expectations and obligations clear. There will

ALWAYS SIGN ON A DOTTED LINE

undoubtedly be misunderstandings over the course of a collaboration; but if you've taken the time to review expectations in advance, they won't be about due dates, overages, or expenses.

A contract is also a signifier, telling all sides that this is a serious endeavor between two mutually respected parties. **For creative types, few things foster as much confidence at the start of a project** and few things do the opposite as quickly as a client's reticence to sign a contract.

If you don't have an attorney or a legal department, let your creative team draw up the document. It will almost certainly be simpler and more to the point. But regardless of who crafts it, the contract should include project scope (all services and deliverables included), fees, project and payment schedules, number of revisions, expenses, and final product ownership and usage rights. It should also include a "kill fee" in case the collaboration isn't working out and you want out (see No. 59, "If It's Just Not Working"). Hope for the best, plan for the worst.

TELL THE PEOPLE WHO DIDN'T GET THE JOB

NO. 26

TELL THE PEOPLE WHO DIDN'T GET THE JOB

Very few potential clients follow up with those in contention who didn't get the job. Don't be one of those clients. Here are three good reasons why:

1. Because closure. Everyone deserves to have it.

2. Because it's the right thing to do. Telling creatives that we didn't get the job will make us think more highly about you and your organization, improving your reputation and that of your brand and business.

3. Because you never know . . . Our firm once went through an extensive selection process for a large company. We didn't win the job, but the president called to explain her decision, the logic of which I understood. (I wished her well.) Three months later, she called again to ask if we were still interested in the project, which wasn't going as hoped. We jumped at the chance, because her initial display of openness, honesty, and respect told me that it would be a success. (It was.)

BEST PRACTICES WORK BEST WHEN THEY ARE FLEXIBLE

NO. **27**

New clients always want to know what made other projects successful and how to replicate that process—in other words, best practices. But what worked with another company's policies, chain of command, and approvals will probably not be applicable in yours. We tend to follow a process that has evolved over time, but we always adjust and adapt it to each client's needs. Best practices are the ones that will work *in this case*.

But I can offer three general best-practice guidelines:

1. Clarity. If we have a clear brief and terms, we will have eliminated the cause of most problems before work has begun.

2. Communication. If you are open and honest from the outset, we will go above and beyond our obligations. The more we understand your goals, the approval process, and how your company works, the more we will surpass expectations. Give us the information and the space to do what we do best, and you should be very pleased with the results.

3. Courage. Nothing great happens when decisions are driven by fear (fear of failure, fear of losing one's job, fear of looking foolish, fear of getting it wrong . . .). Just keep in mind, even people who do take risks harbor those fears. I'm not saying that every solution needs to be risky. I am saying that you will benefit from a little bravery when encountering a direction you don't expect or haven't seen before.

DON'T WORRY IF YOU DON'T KNOW EXACTLY WHAT YOU WANT

NO. 28

Here's the good news: It is really and truly not your job to know—or tell us—what you want. Your job is to figure out—and tell us—the problem you're trying to solve. Our job is finding the solution.

Start by creating a list of adjectives representing the emotions and responses you hope to elicit from our work. Those descriptors will serve as our North Star when we're deciding what we present to you.

It's our job to create something that elicits those emotions and responses—first from you, then from your audience. We explore possibilities not only to find the best solution but also to help identify your comfort level. Something that may help you get more focused is to ask your creative to choose a few past projects and walk you through the original objectives, the ultimate solution and how they got there. You will find both similarities and differences to your project, but doing this may give you ideas for how to frame the problem you're trying to solve.

Some creatives will present multiple solutions, covering a range of possibilities from safe to radical. Others will bravely show the solution they *know* is right. There is no one right way to help you figure out what you want. But all good creatives will try, and your only obligation is to respond honestly.

WHAT IF YOU HAVE A GOOD IDEA?

Tell us! My saying that you don't need to come up with a solution doesn't mean I don't think you have good ideas. So feel free to share something that you think could work. At worst, it will tell us what type of solution you are imagining. Most creatives will explore that idea and, if it makes sense, try to make it work. Win-win. But keep in mind that we creatives tend to look at things differently than non-creatives. Most clients respond to things that they've seen before, because it gives them comfort and confidence. On the other hand, creatives—especially designers—gravitate to things they and you have never seen before.

Different is not always better, but better is always different. So while we're happy to hear your idea, remember that you are the expert at your job and we are the expert at ours. You hired us for that expertise, and you should trust us if we don't recommend your idea as the best direction. We only ask that you be as open-minded with our ideas as you'd like us to be with yours.

If you really do know what you want, tell us that up front. Or tell us that this is the idea to beat and we have one round to try. It's much better to know that before we begin to work, rather than after we struggle through trying to better an idea that in your mind can't be beat. Some firms may not want to accept that arrangement, but better to allow us to decide if we can make your idea work—or if you should find someone else who can.

SHOW-AND-TELL

NO. 30

It's one thing to know what you like, and another to communicate those preferences to your creative partner.

Communicating your preferences early will save time and money, while sparing everyone those awkward "first date" moments when common ground feels elusive. A creative person will want to know what you find pleasing, effective, off-putting, or ineffectual. As crucial as it is that you let us know what your brand stands for, it is equally important to let us know who you are.

One client of ours captured her favorite things with her phone's camera, showing them to us early in the process. She took assorted pictures of anything that caught her eye: street ads, art, wallpaper in a restaurant bathroom, a vintage travel poster hanging in her home. We immediately saw that those images shared a muted palette and a refined elegance, aesthetic leanings that became even clearer after we talked about what she showed us. Although our final design didn't actually incorporate anything she'd photographed, the overall aesthetic in her collection of images informed the direction we took and allowed us to start on common ground. We were collaborators from the start.

Reference images can also help where words fail—especially valuable in architectural or interior design projects. Understandings of what constitutes a "modern" look may differ, but concrete evidence of what you are picturing puts everyone on the same page.

Another client was equally effective at communicating her taste with a short list: "Everything Apple does, the branding for President Obama's campaigns, and the New York City subway signage." These examples told us that she liked straightforward, clean design—bright primary color palettes with little ornamentation. Chances are she would not have had the vocabulary to describe it like that.

One last thought on this subject: If you're struggling to articulate your aesthetic, your creative team can construct "mood boards" for you to respond to. Some firms even do this as a regular part of their process. A mood board is a collage of photographs, illustrations, materials, ads, and words that evoke a particular style or emotional response—and each one represents a different potential design direction. Their very purpose is to start a conversation about what feels most appropriate to you, generally speaking.

CUT OUT THE MIDDLEMAN

NO. 31

CUT OUT THE MIDDLEMAN

Large creative agencies often have a role called Client Coordinator (a title I loathe). Do you need to be coordinated? To be sure, projects require producers and strategists who are on top of every detail. But make sure that you also get to speak directly with, and express yourself to, those who are doing the actual creative work. **You don't want your words translated by a coordinator** all the time because something important could get lost in translation. After all, we're trying to thread the needle to find the perfect solutions to a long list of objectives, restraints, and considerations. How you communicate this information—both the casual and formal conversations about the project as well as your culture and insights— is what will lead us to the right solution. The more direct those conversations, from client to creative (and vice versa), the more effective they'll be.

Weirdly, such lines of communications are not always available. Many publishing houses, for example, don't allow authors to talk to the person designing their book cover. Sometimes, cover designers don't even get to read the book! This makes no sense to me. Just one chat could spark the perfect insight that translates into the all-important cover. Perhaps the publisher—who is the actual client—doesn't want the author to interfere in the process, give a specific direction that doesn't work, or fall in love with an impossible-to-execute idea. But if everyone is honest and transparent and understands that the publisher has the final say, there should be no problem. The possibility of a better cover should push everyone to have as many creative conversations as possible.

Think of yourself as the author. We need to hear the words directly from you and your fellow decision makers. You understand your hopes and dreams better than anyone else.

WHITE SPACE IS YOUR FRIEND

NO. 32

White space is a design term that suggests "negative space"—aka space where there is no design element. It can work on a purely aesthetic level, but it also serves to tell the viewer where to look, what the hierarchy is, where to take breaks. It can also help an entire piece be more inviting.

A website, ad, or brochure that is chock-full of color, imagery, or type can be difficult to look at and read, let alone understand. Think of it this way: If someone throws a single tennis ball at you, you might catch it; if someone throws ten, chances are you won't catch anything. Sometimes I wonder if people think that if there is too much white space, they're not getting their money's worth. Every piece of available space should be filled, right?

Wrong.

Do not be afraid of white space. It serves a valuable purpose.

And while I'm at it, here are responses to seven other design misconceptions that can regularly trip up clients, hurt the collaboration, and weaken the final product.

1. Your logo doesn't have to be big to be seen.

WHITE SPACE IS
YOUR FRIEND

2. Red is not the only color that stands out. Color choices communicate emotions and depend on everything else around them.

3. We can't "just sharpen" lo-res images in Photoshop.

4. We also can't "just change the font." At least, not without going back to the drawing board. Typeface choice and how it's used affects everything else.

5. If it looks small on your screen, you're probably not seeing it at the intended size.

6. Just because we can use all the colors in the world doesn't mean we should.

7. Yes, we really do need the "copy" (words) to start designing. It can be rough copy, but meaning affects design decisions.

LET THE CREATIVES DRIVE THE FIRST PRESENTATION

NO.

The first meeting at which work is presented is often more pressure-filled than it needs to be. We have all been using words with each other and now we are all going to discuss how those words got translated into vision. Let the creative team drive the proceedings.

Some of us will recount things that were discussed early on. Let us. It will tell you how we arrived at our solutions.

Some of us will offer radically different solutions to the problem presented. Let us. There are usually many different and effective ways to achieve the priorities outlined in the brief, and we may want to gauge your responses to several of them.

Some of us will want to present straight through while you hold back responses until the end. Let us. Let us present however we feel most comfortable, because that will give *you* the best opportunity to truly understand our thinking.

Really, make an extraordinary effort to just listen.

Presenting is a kind of performance. Much as you wouldn't interrupt a singer to tell them they sang a note out of tune, wait to tell a creative that you don't like that one aspect of the whole. You'll get your chance to respond. And when you do, the best initial approach is to ask questions.

Why did you use that color?

Why so much text?

Why did you start with that image?

The idea is to get more information about things you don't understand before you decide what you think. You want to make sure raw emotional responses don't prevent a beneficial problem-solving discussion. How you *feel* matters, but what you *think* matters more.

Focus (at this stage) on the intent of the design rather than the execution. Once you agree on the intent of each solution (the *why*) you can talk about the specific execution (the *how*). But it's very crucial (and very helpful to the process) to separate those two aspects of the work and address each independently.

One more thing: When multiple solutions are presented, clients often ask, "Am I allowed to ask which is your favorite?" The answer? "Yes!" But only after we hear your feedback. We're not being coy. It's just that the dialogue around the presentation might inform our choice, and we don't want that information to be influenced by our opinion.

BE A FAIR JUDGE

NO. **34**

Sometimes, when given the role of design critic, especially for the first time, people think that criticism is required. And sometimes it is. But please keep in mind that your main goal is to collaborate with the creative to make the work better and not to be critical for the sake of it. To that end:

Don't be hypercritical to get your money's worth.
Some clients will give lots of notes even when they love everything. You need only relate actual concerns, because if you think the work is terrific, you've already gotten your money's worth.

Don't worry about the work solving absolutely everything (it never will).
This often surfaces when designing logos. Consider a successful company that's always had branding that is neither offensive nor communicative. They grow big enough to hire a professional designer to create a real identity. When judging the new logo—despite approval from everyone in the room—there is suddenly concern about whether it accomplishes everything. The goal is to solve the most important objectives, and then let time and successful business stewardship imbue the brand—and the logo—with everything else.

BE A
FAIR JUDGE

Don't doubt your opinion.
Be brave and go with your gut—you know your
company, the project, and, most important, what you
do and don't like. For one thing, you have no choice.
You're the final judge. Of course, if you can't commit to
one direction at this particular moment, say that. The
creatives spent a lot of time thinking and tinkering, so
it's understandable if you need more space to consider
all the angles.

A smart client once told me, "I like the first idea right
now, but I think I'll like the second idea tomorrow, so
let's go with that one."

QUESTION EVERYTHING

NO. 35

QUESTION EVERYTHING

Every industry has its own supersecret language and handshake. Designers (and other creative types) are no different. We tend to forget that whatever specialized knowledge we possess isn't shared by all. So if we throw around the word *responsiveness* or assume you know the difference between PMS, CMYK, RGB, and Hex colors,* slow us down and ask us to explain ourselves. Sometimes there will be a technical reason for why a certain direction will save time and money. We know that because it's our job to know. There's no way you would, though, unless you ask us to break it down.

So ask a lot of questions, as often as you like. **Asking questions doesn't make you seem stupid.** It makes you seem like you want to understand things better. Pretending you know everything? Well, it can cause

---

*PMS refers to the Pantone Matching System, a color system consisting of thousands of numbered swatches, used in printing. It allows designers to specify an exact color that will be clear to whoever is producing or printing the job. They are sometimes referred to as spot colors.

CMYK refers to Cyan, Magenta, Yellow, and Black. These four colors, when combined in different amounts, are the basis for printing all full-color images. And, yes, I know it seems like it should be CMYB, instead of CMYK. But the K likely stands for "key," to represent the key plate, which is black. Also, using a K means there's no chance the color will be confused with Blue.

RGB refers to Red, Green, Blue. It is the color system for video and computer monitors. There is a subset of 216 RGB colors considered safe for monitors, but even when using those some colors change from monitor to monitor, thus affecting the final visual experience.

Hex colors refers to three-byte hexadecimal numbers. It's another way to represent RGB colors in programming code.

you to make stupid decisions, at the least. If you don't understand why we came up with the solution we did, how will you possibly be able to explain it to the next guy, or your boss, when they have the same questions you do? More important, for our selfish purposes, I've found that not understanding often leads a client to say no. Chances are, though, that if we can help you make sense of what we've done, we can change your mind. But we can't know what's confusing you unless you ask us about it.

BE OPEN TO THINGS YOU DIDN'T IMAGINE

NO. 36

You were expecting a big, powerful presentation, a solution that shouts your message throughout the land. But you hear only whispers. Or perhaps you thought subtlety was the way to go, and what you got instead was bold type in a thick red bar.

So . . .

Take a breath.

Or two.

Or three.

Don't dismiss the curveball outright just because it wasn't what you had in mind. Surprise may be your first reaction, but it shouldn't be your last. **Don't decide anything while you're still surprised.** Let the work sink in, then consider its potential only after its newness has worn off. While you're recovering, it may help to ask the designer to explain her thinking again. Voice your concerns and let her address them.

Someone said great architects don't build great buildings, great clients allow great buildings to be built. Change the nouns and verbs and the same goes for any creative profession. You make what we make possible, but when the solution is not what you expected, be open to the conversation. The situation calls for dialogue, not dictation.

To me, the best solutions break all the rules, all the preconceived notions of what they should be. As the old *Saturday Night Live* character Stuart Smalley (played by the Honorable Al Franken, U.S. senator from Minnesota), liked to say, "Don't should all over yourself." ("Should" is a terrible driving force.) Those who do are likely to miss out on creating something great—or to prevent greatness from happening.

The noted entrepreneur and bestselling author Seth Godin says that the reason it's difficult to learn something new is that it changes you into someone who disagrees with the person you are. That's scary, particularly to those of us who like who we are. But questioning your beliefs keeps you growing, into not just a different version of you but a better one.

DON'T SAY THAT, SAY THIS

NO. 37

DON'T SAY THAT, SAY THIS

Sometimes it's not what you say but how you say it that derails a collaboration. Bluntness, specificity, vagueness—all of it can get in the way. So . . .

DON'T SAY: Make it red.
DO SAY: **I wish it were bolder and stronger.**

DON'T SAY: Make it bigger.
DO SAY: **I wonder what this image would look like if it were more prominent.**

DON'T SAY: Use a handwriting font.
DO SAY: **I like the feeling of handwriting.***

DON'T SAY: I hate it.
DO SAY: **Can you explain this to me?**

DON'T SAY: What I'm looking at makes no sense.
DO SAY: **Can you explain why you decided on this direction?**

DON'T SAY: Can you try again and make it different?
DO SAY: **I wish it were . . .**
              [whatever you wish was different].

---

*Real handwriting is amazing and beautiful and can communicate sincerity and (sometimes) urgency. Handwriting fonts tend to do the opposite. They are clearly, ironically pretending to be something "real." There are a few good handwriting fonts, but the tell is when each letter is exactly the same every time. That is never the case with real handwriting.

DON'T SAY: I love it [if you don't actually love it].

DO SAY: I think I really like it, but I need some time to gather my thoughts.

DON'T SAY: Here are the changes we want you to make.

DO SAY: Great effort, but there are some concerns we'd like addressed.

DON'T SAY: We need you to do it like this.

DO SAY: We are hiring you to do what you do, so please tell us how you'd like this to work.

DON'T SAY: What do you charge for a logo?

DO SAY: Here is what we are looking for and here's our ideal timeline. Please come back to us with a proposal.

DON'T SAY: It's a little job; there's no need for a contract.

DO SAY: Would you like us to supply the contract or would you like to?

DON'T SAY: We want it to look like this.

DO SAY: Here are a few examples of work we like and think is relevant.

DON'T SAY THAT, SAY THIS

DON'T SAY: I'm not a fan of this typeface.

DO SAY: Can you show us some different type treatments?

DON'T SAY: We can't pay you much, but we'll get you great exposure.

DO SAY: This is how much we can pay. We hope that works for you.

DON'T SAY: This isn't what I pictured, so I don't think it works.

DO SAY: Let me live with this for a day or two.

DON'T SAY: I showed your work to my friends last night at dinner, and they didn't like it.

DO SAY: I was talking to some colleagues and they brought up some issues I'd like to discuss with you.

DON'T SAY: We need this project to accomplish these eight goals.

DO SAY: This is our most important goal, but there are secondary goals we'd love to achieve as well.

DON'T SAY: Can you combine this version with that version?

DO SAY: **This is what I like about this version and this is what I like about that one. What can you do with that information?**

DON'T SAY: Have you designed aseptic baby food packaging before?

DO SAY: **Can you share other jobs you've had that are relevant to this project?**

DON'T SAY: We like both of these ideas, so we'll do an A/B test with them.

DO SAY: **I like both of these ideas, but let's go with this one.**

BEWARE OF GARANIMALS

NO. 38

Designers often present more than one idea. We do this for many reasons, but here's a big one: We have a few directions we like, but because it's our first time working with you, we can't predict which will work best for you. (Don't worry—we'd never show you a direction we wouldn't be happy for you to choose, even if we prefer another one.)

The downside of this strategy is that **sometimes clients see the various options as comprised of mix-and-match pieces instead of the coherent design whole each one is.** Of course, we know that clients will invariably like certain aspects of each idea, and describing what you like and don't like in terms of specific elements of particular design schemes is a worthy discussion to have. The problem occurs when you want us to take part of one and combine it with part of another. It creates a Garanimal, where the new solution is weaker than either original. (You're familiar with Garanimals, right? Those color-coordinated but mismatched pants and tops that were a staple of kids' wardrobes in the early '70s?)

Imagine using ingredients from different recipes because you love each taste in a certain dish. You already know that mozzarella and basil will probably not taste good in a Szechuan curry. Imagine how a designer will feel about randomly combining elements that each work well in their own context to create a weird, contextless mishmash.

Instead, allow us to consider your opinions about the strengths and weaknesses of each design, and let us create a new solution that may not incorporate all of your favorite elements but will nonetheless achieve the effect you are looking for. You don't want a cut-and-paste job; you want something greater than the sum of the parts.

Here's a perfect example of the Garanimals problem. At a brand identity presentation I gave at a production company, half the people in the room liked one logo that my team created, while the other half liked a different one. What they managed to agree on was that the two ideas should be combined. A terrible idea. They didn't understand that they were responding to the logos as a whole, not to their individual elements. After considering their responses to the presentation, we designed an entirely new option. When the once-divided room saw the new idea, they appreciated the differences in the original choices and agreed to go back to one of those. It remains the company logo to this day.

Another encounter with the Garanimals problem didn't work out as well. We were asked to come up with a new retro look and feel for a seaside hotel. We worked with an illustrator to create old-fashioned paintings of the building and designed a logo and typographic system that felt equally vintage. It was a beautiful package, if I do say so myself. When we had finished designing almost everything, the client told us they had just decided they wanted to keep their current very modern logo after all, and asked that it be put on all of the new material. Surprise—it didn't work; the elements contradicted each other. We strongly recommended creating a whole new campaign around the original logo or going with the "vintage" campaign we had produced. They decided to do neither. It was a huge waste of time and money.

Of course, there are cases in which a detail from one design solution can be incorporated into another. But **I promise it's almost always better to consider creative solutions as they were meant to be—as a whole.** What works for dressing children doesn't work for dressing your brand.

AN IMPORTANT NOTE ABOUT GIVING FEEDBACK

NO. 39

Being a good client is not synonymous with being an "easy" client. In fact, oftentimes it's the clients who challenge and question designers who get the best results. **You can be opinionated and assertive** and probing and still be the ideal client. That is what makes collaboration brilliant.

I NOTICE /
I WONDER

NO. 40

One of the most challenging aspects of a creative collaboration is reacting to the big reveal when you see the work for the first time. The whole room turns to you, the client, seeking words of wisdom. Maybe you'll instantly know what you like or don't like and why, but more often you aren't sure how you feel. Meanwhile, we are at a vulnerable moment in our collaboration, and your response—and how you deliver it—will greatly impact the next phase. **Here is a foolproof way to work through your feelings out loud** while also considering those of your creative collaborator.

Begin with an "I notice _____" statement.

Examples:

> "I notice how powerful that image is now, and you really followed our request for color."

> "I notice you handled the logo in lots of different ways across the solutions. Lots to choose from."

> "I notice how happy this whole presentation makes me."

Fill in the blank with virtually anything you notice about the work without passing judgment (yet). You can even notice that the presentation was comprehensive or that the presenter was excited about the work. And

I NOTICE /
I WONDER

if you can't think of anything, try this: "I notice you guys really put a great deal of work into this presentation." It may feel like you are stating the obvious, but trust me, what's "obvious" to you is valuable for us to hear.

This not only gets you out of an awkward moment, it can be revelatory to both you and the creative, who gleans a lot from the simple articulation of what you see. Maybe they meant to convey something else entirely. Maybe what stood out to you was intended to be a minor element. Maybe they didn't even notice it was there before.

Next, seamlessly move on to an "I wonder _____" statement.

Examples:

> "I wonder what you might have done if I hadn't asked you to begin with that image of the horse."

> "I wonder what this would look like with a different palette."

> "I wonder if we should rethink our hierarchy. What do you think?"

"I notice" and "I wonder" statements allow for the conversation to unfold openly without criticism on your part or defensiveness on theirs. You aren't telling the creative to do something. You're giving him feelings to respond to. You are wondering, not directing. **"I notice" and "I wonder" statements can be the difference between having a constructive creative dialogue and a combative one.**

And yes, feel free to use words that feel more natural to you, like "I can't help but notice" or "What do you think would happen if?" The point is to be conversational, but with constraints that can help keep you in the right lane.

IT'S OKAY TO LOVE SOMETHING RIGHT AWAY

NO. **41**

This may not seem like a problem, but it can confound clients. It gets them thinking that it was all too easy or that they aren't getting their money's worth. Yeah, I know it sounds weird. But in a standard project, with a process that includes two rounds of revisions, even the best client might be hesitant to admit in the first presentation that we nailed it.

So think of immediate success as a reflection of how well you briefed us—and how well we connected with your needs as you expressed them.

That's cause to celebrate! And reason to move on.

WHAT TO DO WHEN YOU KIND OF HATE WHAT YOU SEE

NO.

This can happen, even with a fantastically talented creative. But how you offer your reaction will make a big difference in what happens next. So try not to give in to the urge of an automatic no.

Instead, start by asking a lot of questions, especially if we haven't sufficiently explained our thinking. Try to understand what you are looking at more completely. Asking why we chose that particular photograph or those specific colors may help you see advantages to an approach that you might otherwise miss. Even if you hate the execution, you may very well fall in love with the intent.

Consider also that you might be responding negatively simply because you are surprised. The human brain is an expectation machine, which has evolved to make decision-making as easy as possible by confirming what we already know (or believe) and discounting what is new or unfamiliar. In other words, sometimes the best ideas take a little getting used to (see No. 36, "Be Open to Things You Didn't Imagine").

One way to handle immediate disappointment is to just **be honest and say you're not sure if it's working for you,** then ask for time to think about it. Maybe you'll feel differently the next day, after you separate your expectations from reality. Maybe you won't—but you'll have a clearer head with which to explain your issues.

Another tactic in the moment is to begin talking about some tiny aspect you like—a typographic choice, the pacing, anything. Ask yourself, or us, why you like that thing. Why does it speak to you? In addition to softening the blow, finding one area of agreement is a good first step on a journey forward.

SO YOU THINK YOU CAN MAKE IT BETTER?

NO. 43

SO YOU THINK YOU CAN MAKE IT BETTER?

Although the impulse is understandable, it's important to remember that you're not the creative. I often make it a point to ask clients to communicate the goal rather than identify even one possible solution. For example, I'll say, **"Don't ask me to make it yellow. Tell me you want it to be sunnier."**

I promise I'm not trying to stifle your creativity. But if you communicate what you're trying to achieve rather than offer a specific solution, you give us room to do our job. Maybe a change in color isn't the best solution. Maybe using yellow would make the copy more difficult to read and recede on the screen. So maybe we change the background image or redesign the typography instead. Requesting a design that feels more upbeat allows us room to explore—and actually make it look sunnier.

WHAT IF YOU DON'T KNOW WHAT YOU THINK?

NO.44

WHAT IF YOU DON'T
KNOW WHAT YOU THINK?

At some point in a creative process, you're likely to find yourself in one of the following situations:

1. You like something but worry it's not actually good.

2. You don't like something but don't know why.

You hired us, in part, for our level of taste and ability to differentiate between good and bad and the gray areas in between. But we understand not having the words to articulate why you do or don't like something. Just tell us that.

We'll ask you a lot of questions to help you speak in full paragraphs, guiding you through the discomfort to reach a conclusion we can work with. **Even if there are no specific conclusions, talking about it will help us respond.** We will ask more questions, maybe look at some other work together, and try to understand more fully how you're feeling.

Remember this: There is no single right or wrong answer. Coming up with the solution that works for you and the project is the goal. Work with us to get there.

And keep your eyes on the prize—a successful collaboration. Either everyone wins or no one wins. Together we can make it better, if you give us the room to do it.

GIVE ALL FEEDBACK AT ONCE

NO. 45

GIVE ALL FEEDBACK
AT ONCE

I have a client who sends me an email every time they chat with someone else about the project. They introduce new thoughts, new changes, new perspectives. As you'd expect, some of the ideas are interesting food for thought and some are terrible. That's okay—separating the signal from the noise is what we do. But no feedback is helpful if it comes in dribs and drabs over the course of a week.

It makes no sense for us to begin revisions after a presentation until we have all your comments. Otherwise, we'll just be waist-deep in a reactive and inefficient two-steps-forward-one-step-back process. Deliverers of piecemeal feedback appear indecisive or undiscriminating or both. It's pretty clear to us that they aren't thinking that much about what they are sending along. They certainly aren't comparing new comments to previous ones to see if they contradict each other or even support the same goal. Which unintentionally leaves the decisions up to us.

It will be much better to tell us it will take you a week to gather feedback from each of the stakeholders and then put it all in writing for your own review. Then you can be sure that all points are valid and there are no contradicting directions. You then weigh all the opinions and decide which are worth our consideration. This is no small responsibility.

One tossed-off comment that you didn't even feel so strongly about can mean days of work for us. On the other hand, if it's a serious comment with a real possibility, it will be well worth the exploration.

Here's another pitfall: **The greater the number of emails we have to field, the greater the chance of something important getting lost in the shuffle.** (I know you know what I mean.) If instead we have one email to work from, not only can we use it as kind of a checklist but it will also give us a chance to consider how all of the comments will work together and propose thoughtful solutions about our next steps.

My favorite way to receive feedback is a combination of a phone call and a follow-up with a written list, from you or us. The call is necessary because we all get to be heard and have the opportunity to ask questions and make comments. The list is crucial because it summarizes what was discussed on the call and what we think was agreed upon. You don't want to rely on any one person's memory for a call because sometimes people walk away with different conclusions.

I tell my designers to follow my feedback precisely and *then* also do what they think is right based on how the work is shaping up. We do the same in turn with clients.

Maybe you really want us to add a floral element, but when we do it, we know it isn't working. We'll show you what you asked for, and then show you what we think could work better, keeping your desired effect in mind.

Another difficult situation is when clients change their mind after giving a go-ahead. Think of it like a construction project. After the ground has been broken, it is expensive (and wasteful of time and energy) to go backward, reconsidering what has already been built. It also messes with our heads and throws the possibility of a single-vision creation out the window.

That said, it can and does happen even with all the best intentions in place. If you preface a change of direction with an acknowledgment of the emotional toll of the change, whatever follows will go down easier.

WE DON'T CARE WHAT YOUR SPOUSE THINKS

WE DON'T CARE WHAT YOUR SPOUSE THINKS

The call from the client typically goes something like this: "I showed my husband/wife/partner/son/daughter/ second cousin what you did—they know much more about this stuff than I do—and he/she/they thought we should go in another direction."

While we are sure that your life partner and/or progeny are wonderful people with excellent taste—and maybe even do know "more about this stuff" than you do—what you show them is likely their first interaction with the project. They haven't read the creative brief, heard you discuss the project with us or your colleagues, had any conversations with us, or attended the meeting at which we explained our thinking. So hearing from them is more than a little frustrating.

Don't get me wrong. Their opinion is valid because it's their opinion. Everyone has new thoughts and perspectives that come at random, even inconvenient times. (Sometimes I wake up with different solutions to projects long complete. This is not a discouragement of new ideas or directions or thoughts.) Moreover, the opinions of those close to you are even more relevant if you, the client, truly believe they have brought up interesting points. So once you discuss your loved one's thinking with your colleagues and any other relevant stakeholders, you are welcome—even encouraged—to raise any points that survive that gauntlet with your creative professional.

We ask only one thing: Don't tell us it came from your spouse!

Own it. Don't bring up the mister or missus. **Instead, explain it to us in light of the original brief** and all the conversations we've had. Because few things are more frustrating to a creative (or anyone, I would imagine) than the idea that all our hard work—not to mention our collaboration with you, dear client—can be undone by dinner table or pillow talk. It's maddening, and it can quickly undo the trust we've built together.

Oh, one other thing: If you tell us that your spouse had a new idea, suggesting that we now follow this new direction, well, we now have a new de facto client. So it's only fair that we meet with said spouse, and that he or she attend meetings going forward.

Won't that be fun for everyone?

ON FEAR AND INSECURITY

The emotions that drive creatives are hope and optimism. We believe we can make a difference. We know we can make a difference. For you. That is why we do what we do. If we didn't believe in it, we couldn't do it. Too often, the emotion that drives clients is fear and insecurity. When those two sets of feelings get together, there is bound to be dissatisfaction and frustration.

But hard choices are hard precisely because there is no one right answer. That is especially true when working with creative people.

Don't let fear drive. It's an especially terrible driver in creative endeavors. **Fear usually drives people to make the most cautious choices.** I'm not saying you should always go with the riskiest choice, but if your only reason not to do something is fear, you need to step back and analyze it again.

What are you afraid of? What is the worst thing that can happen? Try to put the choice in perspective and understand whether there is a single element that is keeping you up at night—or if it's the whole thing. You are in the driver's seat. If you decide the best solution is to begin again, that's fine. Just make an extraordinary effort to understand what is driving that decision. And make sure you can explain that decision so the creatives can understand and respond effectively.

WHY FOCUS GROUPS SUCK

NO. 48

Truly great work is not achieved by committee or consensus. Great work is achieved by someone with a strong vision or an original idea—and the leadership skills necessary to convince others to take the creative journey with her. They have the support of teams both above and below, people who trust and believe in them. That journey should not pass through the sterile, one-way-mirrored rooms that house focus groups.

It's not that the people in those groups don't take the responsibility seriously. Quite the opposite: An executive at a multinational brand company once told me that Americans really look forward to that decisive moment in the store aisle when they get to choose which box of tissues to buy. So being asked (and paid!) to weigh in on the aesthetic qualities of anything is a pretty big deal to most people.

A crowded table of strangers wanting to do good without really knowing what "good" means as they respond to a facilitator's leading questions is not conducive to creative input. Add to that the fact that in a group of strangers, a dynamic inevitably develops in which a single strong personality articulates a position and the rest of the group follows. The result is that in a room of, say, ten interviewees, you're probably getting no more than a couple of reasoned opinions. That's not a focus group; that's a focus pair.

Worse, **group settings often lead people to mistake criticism for intelligence.** A guy who says, "Hey, that's cool" doesn't seem as smart as those with something negative to say. So critical comments rule the room in focus groups, even absurd insights like "That shade of red is weird." And while many clients understand the psychology at play, it's hard to ignore negative feedback. It's an act of bravery to continue to like that "weird" shade of red after the group has spoken.

And of course, we all know that in real life, the person who will really be respected is the one who is not afraid to be honest about her feelings even if they are not consistent with the group's. That bravery is rare. Watch *12 Angry Men* for the perfect illustration.

George Lois, the legendary art director best known for creating iconic *Esquire* magazine covers, famously said, "Great ideas can't be tested. Only mediocre ideas can be tested." That's because most of us don't have the framework to respond to revolutionary originality (or even plain old originality). Focus groups rate only what the people in them are already comfortable with or what we already understand as being "good." But good design should be distinct and specific to particular client needs. Imagine the advice Apple would have heard had they focus-grouped the packaging of the iPhone: "That sure is a lot of white space." Or "You should put a picture on the outside so I know what I'm getting." Instead, unboxing those first iPhones felt like revealing a beautiful, sui generis object. That experience of delight simply could not be properly valued in a "test" setting. Gathering opinions in a focus group leaves no room for a visionary solution or a revolution in design that is not yet quantifiable.

If you insist on focus-grouping a concept, make sure the moderator steers the discussion away from generalizations. Better yet, conduct focus groups before you have a design in order to learn what the public thinks about your company or the product in question or the competition. Established consumer beliefs should inform a creative brief, not a creative solution.

Twelve publishers (about the size of your average focus group) rejected *Harry Potter and the Sorcerer's Stone.* In the end, what it took was one person of vision— the thirteenth publisher, who considered the idea independently, rather than based on the consensus of a roomful of random people—to turn one woman's brilliant idea into a global phenomenon.

DON'T LET DATA DRIVE YOUR DECISIONS

NO. 49

The data we all now have access to is so cool, but we shouldn't be slaves to it. Successful businesses cannot be run by data exclusively. They'd never keep up with it. But judging creativity or being a slave to the data in creating a brief is even more absurd. Data doesn't have room for a visionary outlook that is not yet quantifiable. It can't anticipate imagination and joy and the role they play.

Some decision makers like to settle creative debates with an A/B test because it relieves them of the responsibility of making the hard choice themselves. But it means that they also miss out on the enlightening discussions that precede decisions, when you can decide on the relationship between A and B and the benefits of each. That's their loss. My loss is that A/B tests don't account for the possibility of impact over time.

Worse, **data doesn't leave room for the most unquantifiable of qualities: vision.** If creativity defeats habit, data testing reinforces it. People tend to respond to the familiar, feeling more comfortable with something they have seen before. But the familiar has no magic. It is known and predictable, and—yes—quantifiable by data. But you are presumably in this for the long haul and want to (or need to) differentiate your brand. Not in a way that alienates, of course, but A/B testing is a terrible way to assess the impact and possibilities of creativity.

CONFIDENT NOT ARROGANT

NO. 50

Confidence is a beautiful thing. It's based on reality—you know who you are, what you're doing, and, most important, what you don't know. Someone who is confident brings out the best in everyone. When you get praise from a confident person, you work harder to get that praise again. When you are criticized by a confident person, you take it seriously because you know they only do so with good reason.

Arrogance, on the other hand, rarely gets you what you want from a creative. It's based on insecurity or fear, both terrible drivers. You (subconsciously?) need to put other people down to give the impression that you, in fact, know everything and everyone else is inferior to you. It never works. When creative people work with someone arrogant, it makes them withdraw rather than strive. **No one wants to be yelled at or scolded,** whether they are five or fifty years old.

With an arrogant person, we tend to ignore both praise and criticism, feeling it is all self-serving. We go about our business doing the best we can to get through and around it. This doesn't create great collaborations or, more to the point, great work. I would try two other modes on for size. One is self-doubt. Question yourself. You may learn something new by wondering, listening, being curious about what others think. The other is empathy. Imagine how we're feeling/what we're thinking. It works wonders in every situation.

PICK YOUR BATTLES

NO.  51

Compromise, that lovely and noble salvager of relationships—how valuable it can be. Especially if we think of it not as "caving" but rather as letting go of something that doesn't matter nearly as much to us as it does to our partner. (An accommodation, if you will.)

Make no mistake: I'm not suggesting that you relinquish your insistence on anything important to you. But when you're dealing with a list of issues and your creative partner feels very strongly about a couple of the items, it means one of two things:

1. We may very well be right; this is, after all, our field of expertise.
2. You will make us happy if you let us have our way every once in a while.

A satisfied creative partner is much more likely to find the best solutions for those changes that you do feel most strongly about. It's win-win: two people concocting a mutually beneficial arrangement from two competing opinions and needs—as if you're the only two people in the world that matter. Because, at that moment, you just might be!

THE
POWER OF
ENCOURAGE-
MENT

A little love goes a long way if your aim is to get the best results. The power of encouragement can't be overstated. Creative brains thrive on psychic payments, so I recommend you heed this advice in good times and bad.

The time span of any creative project provides ample opportunity for a random email praising our work and appreciating our effort. This out-of-the-blue message puts a swing in our step and encourages the extra late-night push to live up to the praise. Also, it costs you nothing.

This approach may feel harder when things go wrong, but even then, carrots are simply more effective than sticks.

Consider the different responses to a difficult first presentation in which, due to miscommunication or misunderstanding, the creative missed the boat by a mile. One client was discouraging and one was encouraging. I've experienced both.

CLIENT NUMBER ONE
"Looks like we might have made a mistake when choosing your firm. We are really disappointed. Contractually, we have to give it another try, but I'm skeptical this will work out."

CLIENT NUMBER TWO
"Obviously, this went badly, but we still have faith in you. We are fans of the work you've done for others. Please consider all we have discussed."

Berating the creative is of no use—especially since the client has nothing to gain from a second failure. Yet that's the likely outcome, as I can safely say it is very difficult to give our heart and soul to a client who doesn't believe in us.

I'm not encouraging false praise. In fact, if that's the only type of praise you can offer, sit down over coffee or a stiff drink and try to figure out how to get the collaboration back on track.

A graphic designer colleague posted a note on Facebook recently that simply said: "Will work for thank-you cards."

I know he's not alone.

ACCEPT THAT EVERYTHING IS EMOTIONAL

NO.

ACCEPT THAT EVERYTHING IS EMOTIONAL

People behave differently at work than they do at home or with friends. More reserved, more "professional"—in short, less human. But their emotions are still there, simmering just underneath the surface.

For creatives, who are doing something that seems a bit mysterious to non-creatives, this is even more true.

Acknowledging and accepting that **emotions are a normal part of the creative process** and the resulting client dynamic will help everyone in any collaboration.

This kind of work requires that we share the inner workings of our brains. Doing it well means we've made an emotional connection with your audience, which we can only do by pouring our emotional selves into the work. Those emotions sometimes overflow, especially—again—if it's not going well.

Our professional persona will try to remain calm and cool, but another part of us—the one that stayed up all night to make it perfect—will be devastated. We may get emotional. We may even cry. And that's okay. It's part of the process.

You too may find yourself more emotional and insecure in these projects. Creative work can seem elusive and confounding to non-creatives. Especially when we are shaping the part of your business that will be exposed to the public. There's an unknown factor, and it's a problem you can't solve yourself. Clients will get more upset with us than other collaborators, especially when they feel it's not going well and their job is on the line. And that's okay too—also part of the process.

TALK IT OUT

NO. 54

Someone once said a creative's work is only as good as the number of uncomfortable conversations she is willing to have with her client. Positive results are dependent on the successful navigation of a variety of fraught topics—expectations, budgets, deadlines—and breaking them down takes guts. From both parties.

So you need to be as devoted to dialogue as we will be.

Talking through misunderstandings, misgivings, mistakes, and whatever other human issues may arise helps to dispel momentum-killing and emotional awkwardness. Not talking through them only makes it worse.

This is not about being confrontational. It's about being conversational.

Yes, it can be frustrating when you ask for a change and the person you're paying doesn't want to make it. But if you don't give us the chance to explain our point of view, how will you convince us? Or vice versa?

So have the hard, honest conversation. Don't avoid emotions (see No. 53, "Accept That Everything Is Emotional"), and don't be afraid to raise fears. Talking defuses emotional impasses, stress, and frustration. And when I say "talking," I literally mean talking. Don't get into email exchanges about important issues; the tone of written messages is frequently misinterpreted, and once the damage is done, unintentional or not, it will be hard to repair. And never, ever start a fight over email; that's like breaking up with someone on a Post-it. Show you care by having a real conversation with a real person—without eye rolling or table pounding or hanging up.

Some people think they will spare our feelings if they withhold the truth, but if you know how you feel, pull the Band-Aid off quickly. It will save time and strengthen our relationship. While it can be scary to tell someone how you feel, take comfort in the fact that the creative likely knows how you are feeling already. We are always reading you and your emotions. The biggest surprise will be your willingness to discuss the feelings. Once you reveal your vulnerability (a universal condition)—someone we're working *with* on a project and not a suit we are working *for*—I promise the results will always be better.

This is a relationship. Invest in it.

PLEASE DON'T PISS ON THE CREATIVE

NO. 55

PLEASE DON'T PISS ON THE CREATIVE

This may sound funny, but the client's need to mark their territory on a creative work for the sake of it happens way more often than it should (which is never). This is why we get requests for a small change that seems to fall under the heading "just because" . . . or a huge change that influences everything. I presume this instinct comes from the client's (subconscious?) desire to feel that they're an integral part of the creative work—to mark their territory. But the crazy thing is that the client has already marked the work in a huge way. The whole project wouldn't be what it is without them. There is no need for this step.

Just be sure to keep your ego in check. Will this change really make the work better? If yes, then great! That's what we all want. If you have a funny feeling in your tummy that you are doing it to assert your authority, then take a deep breath and realize you already have the authority; no need to assert it here. You are the client.

There are a few key warning signs to look for:

> The change is minimal and doesn't really impact the job, but you want it anyway.

> It comes after we have worked through all the major decisions but before you would incur change costs.

You are giving us a directive rather than engaging in a conversation.

If you still believe a change is necessary, **all we ask is that you call us to discuss and deliberate.** Explain your reasoning, and let us think about the suggestion. In the end, it may turn out to be a great last-minute fix.

NOTHING TAKES A SECOND

Clients sometimes ask us to make changes or explore a path that will "just take a second." We can't read minds, so we don't know for certain if they truly believe that what they're asking is as simple as flicking a light switch or if they are trying to downplay extra work so it doesn't feel like an imposition or if what they really mean is "I want you to do something extra, but I don't think this should cost more."

But whatever the actual intent, I'm here to tell you that nothing takes a second. In the request, **we often hear sentiment that's at best dismissive of our time and at worst dismissive of our value.**

That change you think will take no time at all? Sorry, but it will. Everything does. Knowing and respecting that will make a huge difference.

Ask yourself this: How good would the result be if the change did take just a second? Certainly it wouldn't give us the time to put any thought into how the specific change might affect the coherence of the full project. You wouldn't want that. You *shouldn't* want that.

A client once asked us to change a few images in a design scheme, suggesting that it would only take a second. But a raft of factors had gone into choosing the images that made it into the work: color vs. black and white, page balance, subject diversity. We had also designed the typography to complement certain photos; in some cases, the swapped-in photos clashed with the type. We made the changes—we heard what the client was telling us—but it took a lot longer than a second to make the new photos look right.

This too is a two-way street. We're asking you to recognize how much time each task takes, so you can expect us to give you the time you need to consider each iteration of the work. It doesn't help us if you rush past mistakes that you're going to need us to fix later on. So go ahead, take your time—or at least more than a second.

DON'T ASK TO SIT WITH US WHILE WE MAKE CHANGES

NO. 57

I can promise you that we will politely answer no. (Maybe not so politely.)

I can't imagine you would like it if someone sat behind you while you wrote a report at your desk, chiming in every once in a while with a "helpful" suggestion. Neither do we.

Clients generally propose this scenario figuring that it will save time. "We could eliminate the back-and-forth," they say. What it will also eliminate is our ability to do our job well. That often involves creating hundreds of ugly things before the beautiful thing comes along.

You do not want to see how the sausage gets made, but the truth is, in this case, you can't. The truly exciting part often happens in our heads anyway. We may need to just sit and stare at the work for a while, spend some time thinking about it. Nothing to see.

Don't take it personally. Designers don't even like their art directors to "sit with them" while they work. There's a photo blog called *Hovering Art Directors*, a living tribute to that awful moment when art directors stand behind designers and tell them to make a change while they are being watched. No one can use their creative brain fully when someone is putting pressure on them to "create." No one.

DON'T FALL OFF THE FACE OF THE EARTH

NO. 58

DON'T FALL OFF THE FACE OF THE EARTH

Every contract should include a schedule so that everyone knows how much time each phase of the project should take. If the process goes a bit off track, fine. The schedule is just a guideline. As long as we confer about shifting time frames, things should continue along smoothly.

But if that conferring doesn't happen—if communication stops or gets drawn out beyond reason—all bets are off.

Creative professionals—like most everyone else but especially if they're freelancers—schedule their workflow around agreed-upon schedules. When that schedule goes off the rails, it makes it hard to plan for other projects we need to do to make our rent. In fact, we might have turned down work to be available for the agreed-upon schedule. When you ignore the schedule, you are disrespecting our business arrangement. How eager do you think we'll be to jump back in when you do finally call? More to the point, who's to say whether our schedule will allow us to?

Communication blackouts also suck the momentum out of the process. After being put on indefinite hold, it takes time to get back into a project's particular rhythm. There's an emotional toll too. When we don't hear back from you, it's a little like getting stood up. We've worked hard to do the right thing; of course we're anxious to hear what you think of it. But if you don't get back to us within a reasonable time frame, you're kind of saying you don't care about the work as much as we do.

We aren't asking for much. Even a simple sentence of explanation via email will suffice: "Apologies, but we're actually going to need a couple of months to reevaluate everything, so we'll get back to you the week of May twentieth." Another perfectly fine response: "We received the email but won't have a chance to look at it until later this week."

Here's another easy one: "Thank you." That's all we need to know that actually you received what we sent. A simple acknowledgment of effort is worth more than you know. Having to write to a client to ask if she got the stuff we sent a week ago is crazy-making.

Shit happens. We get it. But a quick email to concede that will make a huge difference in the ongoing relationship.

IF IT'S
JUST NOT
WORKING

NO. 59

You're trying to make this work, and the creative you've hired is clearly talented, but something about the working relationship just isn't clicking. Maybe the conversations aren't productive. Or the creative doesn't respond in a timely enough fashion. Maybe you find yourself talking only to junior members of the creative team. Or maybe the work is just terrible. You've begun to dread getting on the phone with them. Maybe you've lost confidence in the fundamental direction of the project.

Those are all good reasons to cut bait. But before you give up . . .

Talk it through one more time. Definitely tell the creative how you're feeling, but do it with empathy for their position and with an honest desire to find a better way forward. They may well have a legitimate, and resolvable, beef. As I said earlier, a good creative can be measured by the number of difficult conversations she is willing to have. You have to be willing too.

Take a look in the mirror. Be honest: Are you sure you've been a good collaborator? Is it possible you've been unreasonable? Have you been pushing too hard? Without realizing it, you might have started to act more like the creative than like a client.

Try shifting your approach. I once had a client—call
her Natalie—whose boss forced her to work with us.
She wasn't happy about it and made it clear that she
didn't like me. And I didn't like her right back. One day
I decided to conduct an experiment: If I really made an
effort, could I make her like me and make myself like
her? So instead of dreading getting on the phone with
her, I looked forward to another opportunity to change
our relationship. I listened more attentively. I did not
take anything she said personally. I complimented her
ideas and approaches.

And it worked! We began to appreciate each other and
even became friendly. And since she now liked me,
she trusted me, and our collaboration flourished. Yes,
it took work and a little swallowing of pride, but it was
worth the effort. (She later hired us herself for many
other projects.) I have since "Natalied" others as well.
Perhaps it's a tactic that will work for you.

Of course, it may be that you've done all you can and
you're still not where you want to be. In such cases,
don't hesitate. Because if you're unhappy, chances
are the designer is too. Hopefully, you've prepared for
the worst and there's a "prenup" (kill fee) in place. If
not, a phone call between reasonable, soon-to-be-ex-
collaborators should yield an amicable agreement.
The creatives should keep in mind that they have

essentially failed you. You should keep in mind that they paid employees to work for you. You hold the checkbook, so you have the power. Err on the side of fairness, not bitterness. Both sides should be equally content (and possibly annoyed) when you part ways.

WHEN CREATIVES ARE ASSHOLES

As much as this book is meant to explain how designers, architects, writers, and other creatives might need special care and feeding to get the best results, I don't have any patience for creatives who think of themselves as "artists" first.

So don't fall for any temperamental genius crap.

I know of one colleague who refused to include a visual remembrance of a client's deceased partner in a project because it didn't fit his design.

Can you imagine? Well, I'm here to tell you that this is not the way it's supposed to work. Clients shouldn't treat creatives badly—and **creatives shouldn't treat clients badly.** But it happens. Creatives are humans, and some humans are mean, manipulative, and holier-than-thou. Maybe they offer one solution and expect you to just take it. Maybe they belittle your ideas or play off your insecurities or refuse to make changes. Maybe they throw things. Whatever the behavior—and this is yet another reason to do your homework (see No. 17, "Call References, for God's Sake")—run at the first sign of assholishness. Life is too short.

DON'T BE RUDE TO MY STAFF (OR YOURS)

NO. **61**

Being nice is one of those things you learned in kindergarten that becomes even more important in a professional, collaborative context. Regardless of what else is going on—in your project, your personal life, or the world—you control how you treat others. Use that control.

Clients usually have the sense to not be rude to senior members of a team. But too often that sense of decency flies out the window when more junior people are involved. It's as though the client thinks those people are working for them. They're not—although it would hardly be okay to treat them badly if they were. They work for us; we work for you. If they screw up, we can fire them. You can't.

I know a private school principal who makes sure she is the one answering the phone when parents of prospective students call for applications. She doesn't identify herself, though, because she wants callers to assume she is the receptionist; she wants to see how they act with people they don't think they have to impress. Or people they assume they are superior to. She can't know how far the acorns fall from those trees, but by the end of the conversation she has a good idea of the kind of values those trees have instilled.

DON'T BE RUDE TO MY STAFF (OR YOURS)

We feel the same way about clients who berate their own employees in front of us. We're not impressed by leaders who bully the people they have power over. It only makes them look less competent as a leader and makes us respect them less. And that has a terrible ripple effect.

No one likes a bully, and since it will make us respect you less, it certainly won't encourage us to go the extra mile for you. We file that information away and know that one day, that anger may be turned on one of us.

That's if we decide to work for you at all. Some people are so obnoxious so early in a process that they never get a chance to be a client. Like the record company executive my partner and I once pitched. We were in the middle of presenting our physical portfolio (that's how long ago it was) to this guy in his office, when his (giant) cell phone rang. Explaining that he had to take the call, he excused himself. That's annoying, but it happens. Right before he closed the door, though, he turned to us and said, "Keep going."

Huh? We were pitching to him! There was no one else in the room! Keep going for whom?

At that moment we knew we'd never work with him. He had revealed that he neither understood—nor cared to understand—what we do. I sometimes think about how funny it would have been if when he returned to the room, we had told him that the presentation went great and he had given us the assignment.

SERVE LUNCH DURING LUNCHTIME MEETINGS

NO. 62

Everyone has too many meetings. It's the number one complaint of Corporate America. I don't disagree, but I'm not going to go there right now. I do think, however, that we should make those meetings we must have as enjoyable and productive as possible. I formally submit this simple request: If you've called people together for a meeting at mealtime, **feed us.**

It's hard enough for a roomful of people to focus and cooperate long enough to accomplish anything. Hunger and its corresponding grumpiness exponentially lessen any chance of accomplishment. So for our stomachs'– and your project's–sake, give us something to chew on.

ABOUT PRO BONO WORK

Creatives get many requests to work gratis for a good cause. Most of us love doing these projects, since it's a chance to make a difference by doing what we love. And equally important and somewhat liberating is lending our talents to an organization whose goal is *not* making money. But the joy will quickly fade if your actions do not reflect—and make up for—the lack of pay. **Pro bono projects should not follow the normal way of doing business,** but rather should be handled with unusual consideration and thoughtfulness. For example, whereas multiple (sometimes unlimited) iterations and presentations are standard in paid creative work, that's asking a bit too much from someone who's doing such work for free.

So it is even more important to strictly follow the guidelines in this book for a wonderful and joyful collaboration (yes, they apply to paid projects as well, but they are of even more importance in these situations). And I would place even more emphasis on giving credit whenever and wherever you can (see No. 64, "Give Credit Where It's Due") and sending samples of the work to the creative so they can show it off too.

With this kind of mind-set, everyone wins.

GIVE CREDIT WHERE IT'S DUE

NO. 64

A while back, we spent a year on a project with a famous person. When the project was finished, and she was interviewed about it, she said she had done the work herself, including the design. It made no sense—she isn't even a designer—but she said it anyway.

Creatives, especially designers and copywriters, are used to being an invisible partner. Companies proudly announce a new identity as though it appeared out of the ether, landing on their desk complete. Rarely do they announce the creative collaboration that culminated in the brand reboot or a new slogan. This has always seemed odd to me. How cool would a company appear if it bragged not only about what it does but also about how they appreciate what others do and work really well to get the best out of everybody they deal with? Instead they go the stealth designer route and don't mention it.

I guess they want you to assume it was done in-house, which I get. But if it was done in-house, even more reason to name names. Mention the creative director as you would the executive who makes the announcement. There's even more reason to acknowledge your own employees. **It creates loyalty** and lets them know they are appreciated. The next time, they'll work even harder and other creatives will be attracted to a company that acknowledges their talent.

GIVE CREDIT
WHERE IT'S DUE

I wrote a nice email to "Famous Person" suggesting how great it would be for our company if the next time she talked about the project, she mentioned that we had worked on it together. I never heard back.

If you're a bit shocked at how badly Famous Person behaved, think back on whether you always share credit on your collaborations. Few omissions are as glaring and public as what happened to us. But quieter oversights sting too.

Sharing credit takes nothing away from your achievement. If anything, it makes you look like a bigger, better person.* To be fair, more than a few clients who appreciate our work and the effort we put into it include us in their press releases (which of course makes them look smart for hiring well and takes nothing away from them).

While I'm on the subject, we'd also like you to allow us to put our link on the website or a credit at the end of the TV show we just helped you with. This will also help you, since more people will be exposed to you, your company, the project, and your appreciation of good design.

---

*This seems like the perfect time for me to thank everyone who has ever worked at Eight and a Half and Number 17.

Some companies not only discourage this but also actually forbid it in their contracts. Fortune 500 companies. The ones that are supposed to lead. Again, I guess it's because they don't want anyone to peek behind the curtain and see the elves doing the actual work. The thing is, we're not elves.

DON'T USE THESE WORDS

NO. 65

Terms like these are often meant to simplify complex concepts, but they can end up complicating simple notions. Also, I find that sometimes people use this kind of jargon to cover up their own lack of understanding or insecurity. So please don't use these words—they make everything overly formal and overly complicated for no good reason.

DISRUPTION MATTERS

ADAPTABLE INFRASTRUCTURES

EMERGENT SYSTEMS

RECONTEXTUALIZATION

SHIFTING PARADIGMS

CORE COMPETENCY

DATAFICATION

SYNERGIZE

LEVERAGE BEST PRACTICES

OPEN THE KIMONO

USE THESE WORDS

WORDS

NO. 66

PLEASE.

THANK YOU.

CAN WE SPEAK PRIVATELY?

GOOD JOB.

WOW!

THANK YOUR TEAM FOR US.

DRINKS?

THIS IS THE BEGINNING OF A BEAUTIFUL COLLABORATION.

XOXO

ACKNOWLEDGMENTS

I am grateful to Lia Ronnen for believing in this book from the very beginning and for being such a great collaborator and client and friend all these years. A huge thank-you to Lisa DiMona for being my amazing agent who made so much else possible. Thank you to Gary Belsky, Leslie Koren, and Neil Fine of Elland Road Partners for their wisdom, insight, and incredible skill. Thank you to Anne Kreamer for her sage counsel and friendship these many years. Thank you to Seth Godin for all of his encouragement and support. Thank you to my besties, Emma Cookson, Judy Goldberg, and Penny Shane; my sisters, Rayna Dineen and Nomi Joy Parker; and my parents, Helen and Steve Siegler. Thank you to my brilliant colleagues who shared their stories with me: Sean Adams, Keira Alexandra, Eric Baker, Matteo Bologna, Stefan Bucher, Brian Collins, Louise Fili, Stanley Hainsworth, Alexander Isley, Jennifer Morla, Kristen Ren, Christopher Simmons, and Ann Willoughby. And a very special thank-you to my partner at Number 17, Emily Oberman, for living through eighteen years of this with me. Lastly and most importantly, hugs and kisses and gratefulness to my incredible husband, Jeff Scher, and our children, Buster Scher and Oscar Scher, for putting up with me and for their constant support, love, and inspiration.

And a final thank-you to all my current and past clients. Every last one of them.